Bare George

Bare George

Claire Crowther

Shearsman Books

First published in the United Kingdom in 2016 by
Shearsman Books
50 Westons Hill Drive
Emersons Green
BRISTOL
BS16 7DF

Shearsman Books Ltd Registered Office
30–31 St. James Place, Mangotsfield, Bristol BS16 9JB
(this address not for correspondence)

www.shearsman.com

ISBN 978-1-84861-493-2

ACKNOWLEDGEMENTS
*This poem is a result of a year-long residency at the Royal Mint Museum
in Llantrisant. My grateful thanks for a very happy residency to Lucy-Ann
Pickering, Education and Learning Manager, Kevin Clancy, Director, and
Graham Dyer, Senior Research Curator. The time and care they gave me
was beyond expectation. I also want to thank Claire Aldridge, Design Team
Leader, and the many other staff in the Royal Mint who showed me how a
coin becomes the tiny artwork in every pocket.
All inaccuracies are entirely my fault.*

Quotes from The Golden Legend, *compiled by Jacobus de Voragine, 1275,
and translated into English by William Caxton, 1483, are taken from the
Temple Classic edition edited by F. S. Ellis, 1900.*

Contents

for Carrie Etter

Bare George

wherever there is room on the ground put either a circular group of busts on pedestals, in consultation, all looking inwards – or else the colossal figure of a man killing, about to kill, or having killed (the present tense is preferred) a beast; the more pricks the beast has, the better – in fact a dragon is the correct thing, but if that is beyond the artist, he may content himself with a lion or a pig. The beast-killing principle has been carried out everywhere with a relentless monotony, which makes some parts of Berlin look like a fossil slaughter-house.

Lewis Carroll, diary 1867

i

The george

When I look at a random sample of men called George –
say King, Meredith, Eliot, Curious, Szirtes –
only one is called a Saint. If a man is a george
for my purposes, he is shaped, designed, cut, valued,
minted in gold and put into circulation, free –
the george* – its picture by Pistrucci shows a George (Saint,
of course) killing a dragon, rescuing a woman.

That's not
my story of men:

> *The skin moves on his muscle, sun*
> *over down land.*

a coin now abandoned. Re Pistrucci: classic
copyist stripping men of clothes as well as women.
I warm to him. He dropped the model's toga – bare George!
Xphrastic art, is that what you're calling this poem?
Pissed Strucci, I say. He knew King George was no soldier.
They were pissheads both. He dared George to find where coins
end – die, the bullet-headed punch, is not to die for
coins, it's to remelt – and to visit the furnace
that I say is famous for women's work.

The Coin According to George Herbert

Death hugged me warmly.
Naturally I baulked,
Wondering what he'd done
And sharp-eyed death noticing my recoil
And fulsome as a son
Patted my hand: Look
All the figures show
This is the way to go.
Oh but the cost a loss of made things makes.
I can't begin to think
How taking us out will spoil…
My dear, it's just the brink
Of brilliant things. You must consider me
And what I do.
Then I knew I'd lost you.

iii
Coin City

Let us suppose that only women mint
make coins give the physical to money
forge the material of spend.

> and they brought him a penny. And
> he saith to them. Whose is this image
> and super-scription? They say unto
> him, Caesar's.
>
> *Matthew 22: 19-21*

Perhaps every coin made by a woman
(be she ever so unlike Mary Queen of Scots)
would be a nonsunt, would carry the inscription:

IAM NON SUNT DUO SED UNA CARO

Now they are not two but one flesh.

iv
The Map Keeper

'This is Debt; nor am I out of it.' Faustus, Marlowe, rewritten

There is a country at hand, Uninhabitable.
We've studied its cartography.

It has vast courts of chaotic limestone. We have no
species of mule to carry us

through that. Our policies, developed in long trying
moments of walling such a place,

are generous. We're tired out by its tribes – to them
our name for it is meaningless –

and we know fractures are being set up as we speak
and giveaways of countries cost.

But we respect Violachicks, women who own it.
We pray no one here suddenly

sees them as skinless (they are skinless) because we feel
they carry invisible slings

and are capable of kicking the not that would hold
them. A lesson: we are misused

into incredulous for the sake of our senate.
Violachicks call the payments

cockpit cash. What does that mean? We see their documents.
Let them stick to the currency

of contrast visiting the border. We keep a city
of mood conservation districts

but though we maintain peace, here is the map and all know
we shake the hand of broke daily.

When we hear the boys say, '*Come on sun, march,*' when it's high
and hot and when they look across to

Uninhabitable's honest holds, we think we've buffered
the current generation of

men who'd mimic explosion itself if we gave them
our map and sent them exploring.

v
No Dragons

The skin moved on his muscle like the sun
over down land.

He wasn't killing the dragon, he was casting,
casting me as

a dragon. Well, what did you think I was?

>   It seemed a giant hag-fiend, churning spite
>   of humble human being, held the ground.
>   George Meredith, *Forest History*

So, no dragons.

I'm a woman with my own furnace. Mine
of good metal.

First, though, you learn in the furnace with leftovers come back
to us, bent bits,

holed sheets of metal too poor to pay for anything. You
will work a heat

of up to 1500 degrees. Come down, soft metal,
explain yourself:

vi
To the Dragon Girls

I am used to you and used by you and I have been through
a trillion

remelts. If I'm left to harden you can never soften
the whole of me.

I have to be jackhammered out of the cooled fireplace
and softened in

the bell annealer. Girls feed me in bit by bit.
Each time I flare

fire flame red wind I smoke the cave with my old bonfire,
harnessing fire

to produce what you need, central to human history.
Ancient practice.

> whereof the king was sorry, and said unto the people: For the love of the gods take gold and silver and all that I have, and let me have my daughter. They said: How sir! ye have made and ordained the law, and our children be now dead, and ye would do the contrary. Your daughter shall be given, or else we shall burn you and your house.
>
> *The Golden Legend*

Whereof not! The king was sorry and said to his people
'I have taken

17

gold and silver and let my daughter go but she will die.
I want her back.'

They said, 'This time she will make the gold and silver for us
or let her burn.

We have obeyed your law and our children are dead.
You made the law.'

So I exchange this hot new money, these silver and gold pence
for every girl

who is sent out by convention from the city, virgin
material

into the rocks, to my furnace where I melt, charge and cast
blanks as myself.

The dragon girls are their own currency here in this mint.
Myth makes value

and takes value. But here she comes, with bare George. No other
men come down here.

And he's naked. Why is he naked? Riding a horse?
Crash avoidance?

vii
The Usual Outcome for Incomers

The taxi's seat belts stick
under blank
ets.

It accelerates till
starburst st
o

mach of silver chassis
is clean o
ver

empty road. New tarmac.
Later, cars
pass

The Earth that is His Flesh

Of S. George, Martyr, and first the interpretation of his name

George is said of geos, which is as much to say as earth, and orge that is tilling. So George is to say as tilling the earth, that is his flesh. And S. Austin saith, in libro de Trinitate that, good earth is in the height of the mountains, in the temperance of the valleys, and in the plain of the fields. The first is good for herbs being green, the second to vines, and the third to wheat and corn. Thus the blessed George was high in despising low things, and therefore he had verdure in himself, he was attemperate by discretion, and therefore he had wine of gladness, and within he was plane of humility, and thereby put he forth wheat of good works. Or George may be said of gerar, that is holy, and of gyon, that is a wrestler, that is an holy wrestler, for he wrestled with the dragon. Or George is said of gero, that is a pilgrim, and gir, that is detrenched out, and ys, that is a councillor. He was a pilgrim in the sight of the world, and he was cut and detrenched by the crown of martyrdom, and he was a good councillor in preaching.

The Golden Legend

ix
To the Goddess Handling my Case

After I'd rolled
my socks down to in-
visible –
shaking, we left
the road. Roots loosened, rain

slipped to beyond
the barn's broken spine,
crow-nest ferns
parted to let
me through. *Leave the green bug*

in its spit. Where
nettle bows to you,
the girl goes.
In hurt country,
you cane the dirt with rain.

Cold air walked up
to that gate – I was
bringing her
external warmth.
I took her instructions.

x
The Coin Maker Explains

And now he yells at her, he's as mistaken as he's bare.
Let me explain.

I always do. (It's kinder to the girl, he's confused her.)
I say to him,

'Not you again, why do you escort them? They choose to come.
They will not die

though they will use dies one day, yes, they'll cut and punch
                                                    such rounds
as buy all goods.

Today I'm taking you, Bare George, inside.'
Huge coil of blank

(stamped) metal is fed to the furnace which erupts in flame
and smoke. *Oh some*

misjudge the angle and the metal almost tips out. I
turn black, the smoke

subsides. She heats me slowly, in her small pieces. She gets
her alloy right.

Sampling metal is put in a crucible. I'm taken
for an assay.

If my composition is right, she will cast my metal;
when I am melt

and poured down the channel, I gleam green yellow with yellow
smoke (my molten-

ness). She is fully suited with shielded face and helmet.
I am drawn through

water-cooled graphite dies and my mechanism of coil
winds and pulls me

out half inch by half inch strip. I'm so heavy when she's bound
tons of me I

feel dead with my coils of thick metal but I look coppery –
cupronickel –

I feed out slow on a track. When I weigh two tons, graphite
dies at the end

sever. I'm shiny and marked with CC. Then wound, scalped a
millimetre

on either side to take off my oxidisation till
I am swarf sharp

ready to roll for blanks. Through the rolling mill I go thinner
and longer. Smart

rollers go at different speeds and now I'm to be blanked.
Giant hole punch

fires one thousand blanks a minute. Those blanks are rough. Rimming
smooths the edges.

The girls don't like the huge blue heavy hydraulic machines,
their constant noise.

I whizz through the blanking machine, 650 per minute.
Loud stuttering.

The machine bang bang bang bangs. Blanks pour out in a river.
The sound of tons

of 10 pees falling, coins moving.

xi
Envoi

Let the revolving days be stamped with this.
Slid on its back mouth open creature
Crumpled
Rearing horse
Bare George
A thousand years from now a woman
Picks her sovereign up
And says: 'How crammed this story is and what
A shallow surface for such sharp relief.'
She doesn't see me there. But there I am.

And in the said chapel lieth the body of
S. George, but not the head. And there lie
his father and mother and his uncle, not in
the chapel but under the wall of the chapel;
and the keepers will not suffer pilgrims to
come therein, but if they pay two ducats,
and therefore come but few therein, but
offer without the chapel at an altar.
The Golden Legend

www.ingramcontent.com/pod-product-compliance
Lightning Source LLC
Chambersburg PA
CBHW021950040426
42448CB00008B/1327